DBT Workbook for Kids

*101 Engaging Activities and Exercises to Help Children
Handle Anxiety, Anger, and Cope with Stressful Situations*

Table of Contents

Introduction Letter to Parents

Dear Parents,

Children come into this world utterly unprepared for the onslaught of emotions they'll have to face. Even as adults, some complex emotions are difficult to process and accept, so imagine how young children feel when exposed to new and complicated emotions like anger, anxiety, or depression. As a parent, you do everything to protect your child from circumstances that could make them feel unhappy, unstable, or unsafe. However, there's only so much you can do; you also have to teach your child how to fight their own battles.

You can soothe them and keep them fed and happy when they're crying infants. When they become toddlers, their emotions start developing, but you are still there to guide them. A considerable transition occurs when they grow older and start going to school, making friends, and starting their academic journey. During this period, you can do your best to protect your child, but you cannot control the external factors of their life, especially when you're not with them. So, despite your best efforts to protect your child from negative emotions like anger, hurt, or sadness, they're likely to encounter a situation that triggers these emotions.

At a time like this, you would want your child to confide in you instead of suffering in secret. Most children express their emotions by acting out because they don't know any other way to communicate these distressing emotions. They lack the skills to work through these intense emotions, so they either misbehave or suppress them. Either way, you need to address the root cause of the problem instead of focusing on the behavior itself.

This is what DBT is all about. Dialectical behavioral therapy for kids is rooted in the idea of balancing acceptance and change. This means acknowledging and validating their emotions and feelings while also encouraging them to grow and change. It aims to teach children the necessary skills for managing difficult emotions like stress, anger, and anxiety by combining mindfulness techniques, emotional regulation methods, and effective communication strategies.

This workbook is simple enough for your child to understand and fill out on their own, though they might need help with some exercises. It is structured to engage children in an age-appropriate manner. It includes colorful illustrations, relatable examples, and step-by-step instructions that make the concepts easy to grasp. You're more than welcome to check on their progress as they work through the exercises. However, make sure you respect your kid's privacy and only review the workbook when they're comfortable sharing it with you.

Introduction Letter to Children

Hello there!

Life can be a bit of a rollercoaster, filled with all sorts of feelings. Sometimes, you feel like a superhero, and other times . . . not so much.

Well, guess what? This workbook will help you with all those feelings so you can understand them better.

Imagine this workbook as your special treasure map, guiding you through the world of emotions. Each activity is like a cool puzzle piece that helps you learn what makes you happy, what calms you down, and what sometimes makes you feel not-so-great.

Here's the super exciting part: this workbook is like a magical mirror that shows you more about yourself. It's all about you, your thoughts, feelings, and your big learning adventure.

Check out what this workbook has in store for you:

- Each activity is like a new game where you can find out cool stuff about yourself – like what makes you smile and feel warm and giddy.

- If you ever want to talk about what you're doing or share your thoughts, your grown-ups are here to listen and give you high-fives.

- No need to rush; take your time with each activity. This is your journey, so explore at your own pace.

- By the time you finish, you'll have super skills to handle times when you're feeling stressed, worried, or even a little angry. How cool is that!

Imagine completing this adventure with a bunch of super tricks to handle your feelings like a pro. You'll be like a feelings superhero! So, are you ready to jump into this world of feelings and start your incredible adventure? You're going to rock it!

Section 1: The DBT Adventure Begins!

Have you ever found yourself angry at a friend, and your mind can't let it go? Well, guess what? There's a magical thing called DBT that can help you control your emotions. It stands for *Dialectical Behavior Therapy*; it sounds super complicated, right? Well, it's not as tricky as it sounds. Think of it as a fun journey that takes you through different adventures where you can gain new skills to manage your emotions better.

Imagine this: you're on a quest, just like those heroes in your favorite stories. You know those times when your anger feels like a fire-breathing dragon inside you? DBT has special tools to help tame that dragon and bring peace to your kingdom of emotions. Think about a time when you felt SO happy you thought you could fly. But then, BAM! Something happened, and suddenly, you're as sad as a droopy flower. DBT teaches you how to balance these ups and downs like a tightrope walker cruising through the circus of feelings.

Imagine you're on a quest to conquer all your bad feelings.

Or have you ever been in a situation where your thoughts are like a big, tangled mess? Like that time, you couldn't figure out a tough math problem. DBT's like a treasure map that guides you through the maze of your thoughts and helps you find the hidden gems that make things clear and easy. Here's the secret: DBT isn't about complicated spells or confusing potions. It's like having a sidekick who shows you cool tricks to handle your emotions. Here's a sneak peek into the treasure chest of benefits and tools awaiting you:

Benefits

- **Emotion Mastery:** Become a pro at handling your feelings like a skilled magician taming wild beasts!
- **Better Relationships:** Unlock the secrets to be able to talk openly to your friends and family.
- **Calm Mind:** Wave goodbye to those stormy moments when your thoughts whirl like a tornado. Say hello to a peaceful mind!
- **Confidence Boost:** Discover the hidden gems of self-assurance (feeling good and sure about yourself) and rock any challenge that comes your way.

Useful Tools

- **Mindfulness Magic:** Learn to stay in the present moment, like a ninja staying still in a forest, and let stress drift away.
- **Emotion Surfing:** Ride the waves of your emotions without wiping them out. Catch joy, let go of anger, and hang onto calmness!
- **Thought Wizardry:** Transform tangled thoughts into crystal-clear ones. You'll solve mental puzzles like a mastermind!
- **Coping Potions:** Brew up strategies to deal with tough times. These potions will be your shield against negativity.
- **Communication Spells:** Cast spells of understanding and kindness to strengthen your bonds with friends and family.
- **Problem-Solving Elixir:** Mix up the perfect potion to tackle challenges like a scientist experimenting with cool concoctions.
- **Self-Care Enchantment:** Craft your own self-care spells, turning tiredness into energy and stress into peace.

In the upcoming chapters, you'll get to master all of these useful tools and get your very own "Skills Treasure Chest" brimming with precious ideas. As you complete each exercise, you'll unlock a new skill. And guess what? You don't have to go through this journey alone. You will have some of the most skilled emotion masters right by your side, guiding you through every twist and turn. Meet them now:

Meet
MINDFUL MIA:

She's like a wise sage who knows the secret art of mindfulness. When your thoughts race like wild stallions, Mia will teach you how to tame them and enjoy the serenity of the present moment.

Say Hello to
WAVE RIDER WYATT

Just like a surfer catching the perfect wave, Wyatt is a pro at riding the highs and lows of emotions. He'll show you how to stay afloat even when life's ocean gets choppy.

Introducing
THOUGHTFUL TESSA:

Tessa's your go-to guru for untangling those knotty thoughts. She'll help you navigate through the labyrinth of your mind and find clarity like a detective solving a mystery.

Meet
EMPATHY ELI

Eli's like a warm hug for your heart. He's the Master of Communication spells, who will teach you how to understand and connect with others, and turn conflicts into opportunities for growth.

These emotion masters will pop up throughout the book, sharing their wisdom and joining you on this journey of discovery. Think of them as your fellow adventurers, walking alongside you as you unlock the treasure chest of skills.

Explore Your Inner Map: Discover Strengths, Weaknesses, and Emotions

These exercises are about uncovering your hidden strengths, embracing growth opportunities, and mapping out a path toward emotional mastery. So, answer these questions to figure out what level you're on:

1. Strength Spotlight

List three things you're really good at. It could be anything from making people laugh to solving puzzles. Celebrate these unique strengths!

1. _____

2. _____

3. _____

2. Challenge Chronicles

Recall a time when you faced a challenge. How did you overcome it?

_____

_____

_____

3. Emotion Explorer

Name an emotion that's sometimes hard to manage. Describe a recent situation where you felt this emotion.

Emotion: _____

Situation:

_____

_____

4. Super Support Squad

List the people who always support you. How do they make you feel better? It's always good to show your gratitude to the people who care about you.

1. _____

2. _____

3. _____

4. _____

5. _____

5. Communication Check

Think about a time when you struggled to say what you were feeling. What made it difficult?

_____

_____

_____

6. Confidence Chronicle

Write about a moment when you felt really confident. What made you feel that way? Use this to tap into that feeling again.

_____

_____

_____

7. Emotion Puzzle

What emotion confuses you? Write down what situation made you feel this emotion.

Emotion: _____

Situation:

_____

_____

_____

8. Coping Quest

Describe a recent challenge that left you feeling overwhelmed. How did you handle it? This is a map to discovering how to cope when things seem difficult.

Challenge:

_____

_____

_____

Coping Skill:

_____

_____

_____

9. Self-Care Snapshot

List activities that relax you and make you feel happy. How often do you do them?

1. _____

2. _____

3. _____

4. _____

5. _____

10. Growth Guide

Imagine your future self as an emotion master. What skills have you honed? What challenges have you conquered? This vision guides your journey.

1. _____
2. _____
3. _____
4. _____

Now that you've filled out these questions, you know your strengths and weaknesses. You can use these strengths and improve your weak points by working through the different exercises presented in the next chapters.

Section 2: Detecting My Emotions and Thoughts

People have lots of feelings and thoughts, and these feelings are always changing. Your day can start out great but end up being terrible, depending on the circumstances around you and how you feel about them. The very intense feelings you have trouble managing can be called your "big" feelings, and the easier feelings can be called "small" feelings. Among these big and small feelings, there are some basic feelings that you're likely aware of, like happiness, sadness, anger, etc. Then, there are secondary feelings or more complicated feelings that not everyone has heard of. This section of the workbook will help you explore all types of feelings and thoughts that come up.

You have many thoughts and emotions, and you should get to know them all.
https://pixabay.com/id/illustrations/emosi-smilies-wajah-seru-senyum-751617/

Emotions and Feelings

You know those times when you feel happy, sad, excited, or even a little worried? Those are feelings! They're like messages from your heart and brain telling you how you're doing on the inside. Just like your face shows if you're smiling or frowning, your feelings show what's happening in your heart.

Sometimes, feelings can be a bit like visitors. Happy feelings are like friendly guests who make you feel like dancing, while uncomfortable feelings are like visitors you might not know well and might want to avoid. But guess what? Even those visitors have something important to say!

Uncomfortable feelings are the ones that might make you feel weird or not-so-good inside, like when you're worried about something. It's like having a little alarm bell in your heart saying, "Hey, pay attention!"

Here's something really interesting: sometimes, you try to pretend those uncomfortable feelings aren't there. It's a bit like covering your eyes and thinking nobody can see you! That's okay to do sometimes, but there's a neat trick. If you actually look at those feelings and try to understand why they're visiting you, *they might go away faster.*

Imagine you have a puzzle piece that doesn't quite fit the puzzle. Instead of hiding it, you look at it closely and figure out where it should go. That's what it's like when you pay attention to your feelings. Your brain gets better at understanding why you feel that way, and it helps you figure out what to do to feel better.

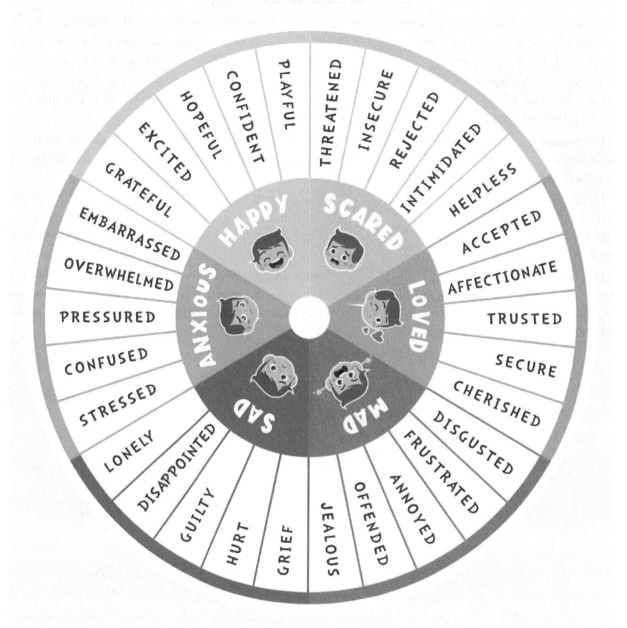

Emotions are like colorful puzzle pieces that help you understand your feelings. Here are some basic ones:

- **Happy:** When you're super excited, and your heart feels like it's doing a happy dance.
- **Sad:** When you're feeling down, and your heart feels a little heavy.
- **Angry:** When you're really mad, your face might turn red.
- **Surprised:** When something unexpected happens, and your eyes go wide like saucers!
- **Scared:** When something spooky or unfamiliar makes your heart beat faster.

• **Excited:** When you're pumped up and can't wait for something awesome to happen.

Now, time to get crafty! Cut out this emotions wheel carefully. Next, grab a sturdy card sheet – you know, like the one you use for school projects. Glue your emotions wheel onto it. Find a toothpick or a tiny stick and stick it through the center of the wheel. Now you've got a spinning emotions wheel!

Give it a whirl! Spin the wheel and see which emotion it lands on. What's that feeling? Happy? Sad? Excited? Write down how your body reacts when you feel this emotion.

Emotion	Reactions

12. Emotion Word Bank

In addition to the basic emotions, there are a huge number of other emotions that you can feel. For instance, do you ever feel confused and angry at the same time? That's called frustration. Or have you ever felt a mix of happiness and sadness at the very same time? That could be described as *bitter-sweetness.* Take a look at this emotion word bank, and familiarize yourself with each emotion.

Calm Happy Interested Excited	Surprised Confused Concerned Nervous Afraid	Cranky Bored Upset Angry Disgusted	Disappointed Hurt Sad Depressed

13. Emotion Story

Read the story on the next page and then answer the following questions to practice identifying the feelings in the story.

EMMA'S NEW SCHOOL

Emma was about to start at a new school. She walked through the front gates with her heart beating fast. The school building was big, and there were so many kids she didn't know. She took a deep breath and headed to the office to get her class schedule.

In the classroom, Emma found an empty seat. She looked around at her new classmates, with her heart beating wildly. The teacher introduced her to the class, and some students waved and smiled at her.

During lunchtime, Emma hesitated before walking into the cafeteria. She wasn't sure where to sit. A friendly girl named Mia waved her over to her table. Emma's face lit up with a small smile as she felt relieved to have someone to sit with.

In the afternoon, Emma joined the art club. She loved to draw, and she wanted to meet other kids who shared her interest. The art teacher showed them a cool painting technique. Emma's eyes sparkled as she tried it out for the first time and saw her creation come to life.

As the school day ended, Emma walked out with Mia. They chatted about their favorite subjects and hobbies. Emma felt a growing sense of comfort and happiness. She knew that even though new things could be a little scary, they could also lead to wonderful experiences and new friendships.

Questions:

- How might Emma have felt when she looked at the big school building and saw many kids she didn't know?

  _____

- What emotions might Emma have experienced when the teacher introduced her to the class?

  _____

- How could Emma have felt when Mia waved her over to sit with her at lunch?

  _____

- What emotions might Emma have felt as she tried out the new painting technique in the art club?

  _____

- How did Emma feel when she was leaving the school?

  _____

14. Emotional Reaction

When things happen to you or around you, your brain gets a message and then tells your body how to respond. Your brain and body are like a team, working together to help you handle your emotions. Complete this table to practice figuring out situations that might make you feel different emotions.

Feeling	Cause	Reaction
Anger	Your friend accidentally knocks over the tower of blocks you were building.	Your face feels hot, you might stomp your feet, and your fists get tight.
Happiness		
Fear/worry/anxiety		
Sadness/depression		

Frustration		
Anger		

15. Big Feelings, Little Feelings

Emotions can be big or small in size. Some feelings are really strong and stay with us for a while. Other times, feelings are like little waves that go away fast. Every time you feel something, it might be a different size or type of feeling. List three small and three big feelings you have felt.

Small Feelings:

1. _____
2. _____
3. _____

Big Feelings:

1. _____
2. _____
3. _____

Your Thoughts

Thoughts are like the words you say to yourself in your mind. Your mind comes up with different types of thoughts. Everyone has three main types of thoughts: feelings, thoughts, facts, thoughts, and thoughts that combine both.

When you have feelings and thoughts, you focus only on how you feel about something happening. It can make situations seem really big and intense, like they're the most important things ever. These thoughts are tricky because they can leave you stuck with thoughts that make you worry about things that haven't happened.

Facts and thoughts are all about what you can see and know for sure. It's like looking at what's really happening without thinking about how you or others feel. Facts and thoughts don't really pay attention to feelings.

When you mix your feelings with the facts, you use *your full thoughts*. This can be tough because you have to deal with uncomfortable feelings and make good choices at the same time. It's a bit like juggling tricky things in your mind.

16. Stuck Thoughts

Sometimes, you may find yourself trapped in your feeling-minded thoughts. Please use the space below to share a situation where you often feel stuck in these thoughts that won't go away.

_____

_____

17. What-Am-I-Thinking Skill

This skill will help you learn how to watch your thoughts without deciding if they're good or bad. It's watching them without getting tangled up in them or paying too much attention.

1. Find a quiet and comfy spot to sit.
2. Close your eyes and take a few deep breaths.
3. Imagine your thoughts are like clouds in the sky.
4. As thoughts come into your mind, don't hold onto them. Imagine them floating like clouds passing by.
5. Don't judge the thoughts as good or bad. Just observe them as clouds.
6. If your mind starts to grab onto a thought, gently bring your focus back to imagining the clouds.

18. Thought Stoplight

Just like traffic lights guide cars on the road, your thoughts can be guided, too. Each traffic light color, i.e., red, yellow, and green, defines a type of thought. The color red means negative thoughts, yellow means neutral ones, and green equals positive thoughts. Now, think of all your thoughts today, and write them down with the correct colored circle.

TRAFFIC LIGHTS

STOP

STOP

WAIT

WAIT

GO

GO

19. Thought Mapping

In the center of this mind map, write down a main thought or emotion you might have, then add related thoughts along the outer circles.

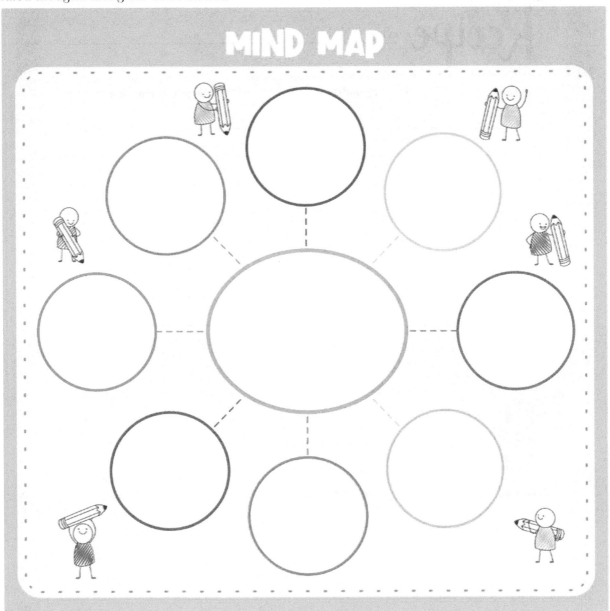

20. Thought Recipe Card

In this activity, you'll be writing thoughts as if they were recipes. Just like when you're cooking or baking, you gather ingredients, follow steps, and end up with a delicious dish. Thoughts also involve different parts that lead to certain emotions.

Recipe _____

Situation	Thoughts	Resulting Emotion
_____	_____	_____
_____	_____	_____
_____	_____	_____
_____	_____	_____
_____	_____	_____
_____	_____	_____
_____	_____	_____
_____	_____	_____

Recipe _____

Situation	Thoughts	Resulting Emotion
_____	_____	_____
_____	_____	_____
_____	_____	_____
_____	_____	_____
_____	_____	_____
_____	_____	_____
_____	_____	_____

Recipe _____

Situation	Thoughts	Resulting Emotion
_____	_____	_____
_____	_____	_____
_____	_____	_____
_____	_____	_____
_____	_____	_____
_____	_____	_____
_____	_____	_____

Recipe _____

Situation	Thoughts	Resulting Emotion
_____	_____	_____
_____	_____	_____
_____	_____	_____
_____	_____	_____
_____	_____	_____
_____	_____	_____

Section 3: Gaining Control of Emotions

Now that you know the difference between emotions, feelings, and thoughts, you can learn to manage the difficult emotions that come up. Every person struggles with one emotion or another. For you, maybe it's anger or stress. For your friend, maybe it's fear. DBT helps you learn emotional regulation.

What's *emotional regulation,* you wonder? Emotional regulation is like having a superpower to handle those pesky little feelings that upset you. It's about learning to manage your emotions to feel better. Just like superheroes practice their powers, you can practice too! Try these exercises to practice controlling your emotions:

You can learn to control your emotions.
https://www.scottbharris.com.au/journal/7-powerful-techniques-to-reframe-negative-thoughts-at-school/

21. STOP Technique

This technique will help you calm down when you're experiencing tough emotions, such as anger or frustration. Try this the next time you get mad at your little brother or sister when they take your toys without asking.

Stop stands for:

S - Stop (pause for a moment)

T - Take a breath (focus on the air going in and out)

O - Observe (what are you thinking about?)

P - Pull back (look at the situation as if you were in a helicopter viewing from above)

22. Emotion Regulation Questionnaire (MCQs)

These questions will help you understand how you react to different situations. Circle the one that is the most like you – AND REMEMBER: there is no right or wrong answer!

When Something Doesn't Go Your Way:

How do you usually react if you can't have something you really want?

- I get really mad and might yell or stomp my feet
- I feel sad and might want to cry
- I try to think about something else or find a different toy or game to play with
- I talk to someone I trust about how I feel

How do you usually handle it when you have to wait for something you want?

- I get really impatient and can't sit still
- I get a little frustrated, but I can wait without getting too upset
- I distract myself by doing something else while I wait
- I remind myself that waiting is okay and try to be patient

When You're Upset or Angry:

When you're really mad, what do you usually do?

- I might hit something or someone
- I might say mean things to others
- I take deep breaths and count to ten to calm down
- I go to my room or a quiet place until I feel better

How do you show that you're angry or upset?

- I show it on my face and let everyone know
- I try to hide it so people don't see how I'm feeling
- I talk to someone about why I'm upset and try to solve the problem
- I draw or write about my feelings to help me feel better

When Something Scares You:

What do you do when you're scared or worried about something?

- I might avoid the scary thing or situation

- I try to act tough and pretend I'm not scared

- I tell myself that it's okay to be scared and ask for help if I need it

- I think of something happy or use my imagination to make the scary thing seem less scary

How do you feel when you're scared?

- My heart races, and I feel really shaky

- I get a little nervous, but I can still do things

- I feel butterflies in my stomach

- I feel safe and comfortable even if I'm scared

23. Coping Strategies Menu

Do you ever feel so stressed about a big school project that you can't bring yourself to start? Or have you ever been so angry at a friend that you want to scream at them? Well, you're not alone. Everyone feels these emotions from time to time, but what matters is how you react to them. If you act on your impulses, you will only create trouble for yourself. Instead, what you can do is find healthy ways to respond to calm you down. Here's a whole menu for you to choose from, and you can add more if you want!

COPING STRATEGIES MENU

WRITE A KIND NOTE

THINK OF A PET

GET A QUICK DRINK

ASK FOR HELP

EAT A HEALTHY SNACK

WRITE A TO DO LIST

MEET A FRIEND

PRACTICE YOGA

ORGANIZE OR CLEAN

PLAY

TAKE CARE OF PLANTS

GO TO A QUIET SPOT

COPING STRATEGIES MENU

COLOR/DRAW

SING
THE ABC SONG

START
OVER

ASK
QUESTIONS

BE
YOURSELF

TAKE
A BREAK

24. Count to 10

Imagine you're playing a game with your friends, and things start getting a little too competitive. Maybe someone accidentally bumps into you, and you feel your temper rising. Instead of getting really mad, you can try a super simple trick. All you have to do is take a deep breath and start counting slowly from 1 to 10. This gives your brain extra time to think before reacting. By the time you reach the number 10, you'll probably feel much calmer and more in control.

25. Safe Space Visualization

If you feel your emotions getting out of control, there's a way you can take yourself out of the situation and into a place you love. *Visualization!* Your imagination is your best friend in situations like these, and there are no rules when it comes to imagining your happy place. It could be a nice beach, a park, or even a magical place filled with candy! In the space given below, draw and color your happy place:

26. Opposite Actions

When you experience an emotion, a reaction comes with it. For example, if you're angry, you'll argue or shout. If you're sad, you'll cry or withdraw from your friends. Everyone reacts to their emotions differently. When you do the opposite of what your emotion makes you feel, you can change your emotion. For example, if you're angry, instead of shouting or arguing, if you talk politely and smile, your emotions can change. Write how you'd usually react to each emotion in this table, and then write the opposite action.

Emotion	Reaction	Opposite Action
Anger		
Frustration		
Sadness		
Anxiety		
Stress		

27. Check the Facts

Sometimes, there will be moments in your life where you will overreact. And when you look back at things, you realize they weren't a big deal. Instead of having to look back and regret your actions, you should take a moment to check the facts about any situation you're in. Ask yourself these questions:

- What happened to make me feel this emotion?

_____

- What assumptions am I making about the situation?

_____

- Do my emotions and their intensity match the facts or assumptions of the situation?

_____

28. P.L.E.A.S.E Technique

Your body and mind are directly linked. An unhealthy body equals an unhealthy mind, which means your emotions will not be stable. To improve your emotional regulation, remember the acronym PLEASE, which stands for:

PL - Treat physical illness

E - Eat healthily

A - Avoid unhealthy habits

S - Sleep well

E - Exercise

29. Positive Thinking

You can get used to focusing on the bad things rather than the good things in your life. However, when you shift to positive thinking, your life will change for the better. So, whenever you're in a tough situation, try to think of the positive side of things. In the same way, turn your negative emotions into positive ones like this:

Situation	Negative Emotion	Positive Emotion
I didn't do as well as I hoped on a school test.	I feel sad and disappointed about my grade.	I am determined to study harder next time and improve my score.

30. The 5-Minute Rule

When you experience intense emotions like anger or sadness, your reactions become uncontrollable sometimes. To avoid this, remember the 5-minute rule. Whenever you feel angry, sad, or disappointed, take a five-minute break from the situation and distract yourself. After some time has passed, you'll feel a lot better about the situation.

Section 4: Interpersonal Effectiveness

So, what's the deal with these fancy "interpersonal skills," you ask? They're the special tools you use to be a super friend and have amazing relationships with others. Imagine them as your social superpowers!

Imagine you have social superpowers!

https://clipart-library.com/clipart/super-mom-clipart-21.htm

- Empathy is like putting on someone else's glasses to see how they feel. If your friend is sad because they lost their favorite toy, you can show empathy by saying, "I understand why you're sad. I would feel sad, too, if I lost something special."

- Validation of others' feelings is like giving someone a high-five for how they feel, even if you feel differently. Let's say your buddy is excited about a new game, but you're not into it. You can still validate their feelings by saying, "I'm glad you're excited about the game!"

- Kindness is like sprinkling friendly glitter everywhere you go. It's about being nice, helping others, and making them feel good. If your classmate feels down, you can show kindness by drawing them a cool picture to cheer them up.

- Forgiveness is about giving your friend a second chance after they make a mistake. If you accidentally spilled their juice, you'd want your friend to forgive you, right? So, if they mess up, try saying, "I forgive you. Let's keep having fun!"

Now that you understand how interpersonal skills work, here are some exercises to flex your interpersonal muscles.

31. The G.I.V.E. Skill

Imagine you have a secret formula for creating strong, superhero-worthy relationships. It's called G.I.V.E., and it's like a magical potion that makes your connections shine! When you value a relationship, remember to:

- **G – Be Gentle:** Use kind words and a friendly tone. Nobody likes a grumpy superhero!

- **I – Act Interested:** Show that you care about what others have to say. It's like giving them a spotlight!

- **V – Validate:** When you validate someone, you're saying, "Hey, I see your puzzle pieces and understand how they fit together!"

- **E – Easy Manner:** Relax - like a sloth on a Sunday. No need to rush, right?

32. The D.E.A.R. M.A.N. Technique

Here's how you can express your needs and wants in a way that's super respectful - both for you and others. Imagine you're writing a note to your BFF and want to make sure it's very clear and kind. Here's the D.E.A.R. M.A.N. technique:

- **D – Describe:** Explain the situation like a storyteller. Paint a picture with your words.

- **E – Express:** Say how you feel and what you need. Let your feelings fly like a friendly bird!

- **A – Assert:** Be confident, like a lion showing its mane. Speak up, but keep it friendly!

- **R – Reinforce:** Show the cool stuff that could happen if your request is granted. It's like a sneak peek into an exciting movie!

- **M – Mindful:** Stay focused, like a ninja on a mission. Don't let distractions get in the way.

- **A – Appear Confident:** Stand tall and speak with superhero confidence. You've got this!

- **N – Negotiate:** Be open to finding a win-win solution. It's like teamwork for superheroes!

33. The F.A.S.T. Method

Even superheroes need to protect their secret lairs, right? Well, you have your own personal space, too, and keeping it safe and sound is totally okay. Here's the F.A.S.T. method to help you out:

- **F – Fair:** Treat others and yourself fairly, like you're the judge in a super cool contest!

- **A – Apologies:** Say "I'm sorry" when you make a mistake. It's like pressing the reset button on a video game!

- **S – Stick to Values:** Remember what's important to you. It's like following a treasure map to your heart's desires!

- **T – Truthful:** Be honest, like a superhero with a crystal-clear conscience. No fibbing allowed!

34. Super Feelings Detective

Grab your magnifying glass for this fun detective game! Pretend scenarios where friends have different feelings, and guess what you might say to comfort them. Say your friend got a low score in a game. What could you say to make them feel better? Here are some scenarios you can try:

Your friend's pet goldfish is missing – comfort them with a kind word and a hug!

_____

_____

Your buddy is nervous about a big test – boost them up with words of confidence!

_____

_____

No party invite for your pal? Tell them they're still a star in your book!

_____

_____

Lost toy blues? Your magical words can turn their frown into a smile!

_____

_____

After a soccer game loss, your cheering words can make them a winner in spirit!

_____

_____

Recess feeling lonely? Your kind words can brighten their day like a rainbow!

_____

_____

35. Friendship Map

Draw a big map with your friends' names and pictures in the given space. Connect each friend with what makes your friendship special, like shared hobbies or favorite activities. This map shows the awesome connections you have!

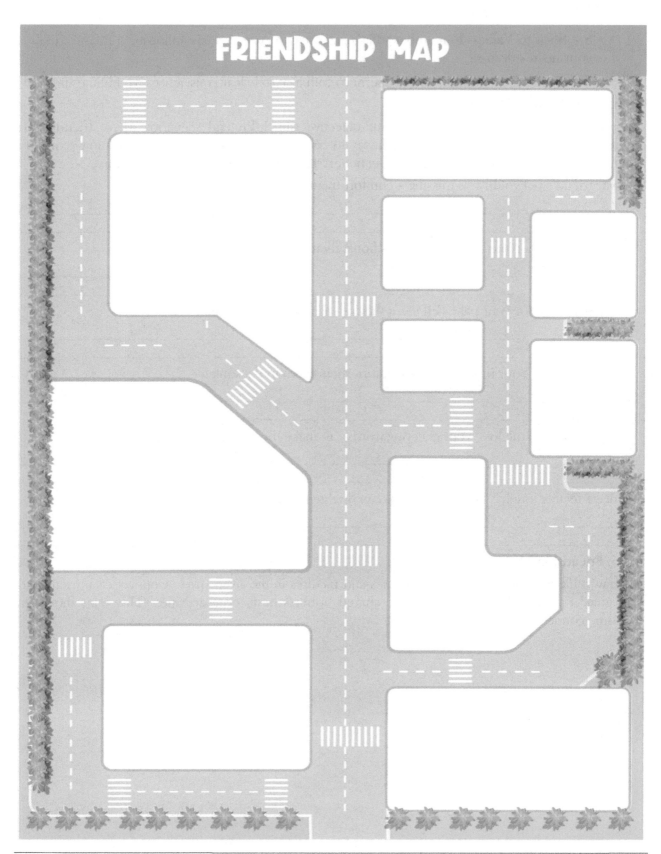

36. Kindness Cards Creation

Design and decorate little cards with kind messages. Give them to your friends to brighten their day. You can write things like, "You're a shining star!" or "Thanks for being an amazing friend!". You can use the templates below to help!

HOPE YOU HAVE
A GREAT DAY

MORE HUGS

37. Friend for a Day Story

Write a short story about being in your friend's shoes for a day. How would you feel, and what would you do? Share your story and learn about each other's feelings.

_____

_____

_____

_____

_____

_____

_____

_____

_____

_____

_____

_____

38. Problem-Solving Puzzles

Here are some examples of problem-solving puzzles!

 PUZZLE TEMPLATE

FIND THE CORRECT PATH

FIND THE WORDS

```
        c t
        h h a n
        w o p r n t
        c n e t d d
        h u e k l o y   y
        l s y b e n e i   i
        j h o t y t u c k n
        n g b l w t t a s e
    c h o c o l a t e d s r
    m l o r t y i m u k k i
    e i n o c k i p e h i d
    p i e i u t a t o a m i
    r c s p t i m p p o
    m a s c l p a c a m
    y k a a h a c o l f
    o e n k m n a o n a
        c t e r c r k h
        m c b k a o i s
        v m h s k o e s
        j j o e n h k
```

cookie	lollipop	honey
cupcake	tartlet	candy
donut	cake	chocolate
macaroon	pie	pancake
eskimo		croissant

42

39. Listening Bingo

Do you like to play bingo? If so, this fun bingo game will be super fun for you. It has listening actions like "nodding," "eye contact," and "asking questions." During conversations, mark off the actions your friend does. A bingo means they're a super listener! Ask them to do the same for you.

LISTENING BINGO

SHOW YOU'RE LISTENING	LOOK AT THE PERSON TALKING	RESPOND APPROPRIA TELY	PUT ALL OTHER THOUGHTS AWAY	NOD YOUR HEAD
ASK QUESTIONS TO UNDERSTAND	PROVIDE FEEDBACK	BE OPEN AND HONEST	DO NOT INTERRUPT	USE EYE CONTACT
RESPOND RESPECTFU LLY	LISTEN THEN THINK OF WHAT TO SAY	FREE!	SUMMARIZE WHAT THE PERSON SAID	LISTEN TO LEARN
DO NOT WALK AWAY	SMILE	LISTEN TO OBTAIN INFORMATI ON	LISTEN FOR ENJOYMENT	LET THE PERSON FINISH BEFORE TALKING
PAY ATTENTION	LISTEN TO UNDERSTAND	DEFER JUDGEMENT	SHARE YOUR OPINION	STOP SIDE CONVERSATIONS

40. Role-Play Theater

One of the best ways you improve your social skills is to practice! Act out different social situations with a friend. One of you plays a character who needs help, and the other uses their superhero communication skills to solve the issue. Try the given scenarios.

ROLE-PLAY THEATER

You were picked to be the captain of your team, now your good friend isn't talking to you because he was hoping to be picked to be the captain.

Half of your friends want to play one game and the others want to play another.

A friend copied your work and got a better mark than you did.

A friend lied to you about what others said about you.

You've been blamed for something you did not do.

Both of you want the same topic for a project and there's only one topic per student.

A friend of yours keeps hiding your belongings and thinks it's funny

Your trust has been betrayed by a friend.

Interpersonal skills are the tools you use to connect with others, like listening actively, sharing thoughts and feelings, showing empathy by understanding others' emotions, speaking kindly and respectfully, solving problems together, and using manners. Practicing these skills helps you build strong relationships and become better friends, siblings, and companions.

Section 5: Building Distress Tolerance

Consider this: You've been practicing your favorite sport for weeks, and the big championship game is finally here. You're excited and ready to give it your all. But guess what? During the game, things don't go as planned. The other team is really strong, and you're losing by a lot of points. It feels super frustrating, and you start feeling upset and even angry.

Now, here comes the important part: It's 100% normal to feel this way when things don't go as planned. Emotions like frustration, disappointment, and anger are like visitors that knock on your door. But you don't have to let them take over your whole house! Learning to cope with these feelings is the same as learning a cool skill. It's like practicing a new move in your favorite video game until you master it. Instead of trying to hide or ignore your feelings, you can learn to deal with them in a more healthy way.

It's normal to feel upset sometimes, but there are ways to deal with this.
https://creazilla.com/nodes/38738-sophia-woman-is-angry-clipart

---

In this chapter, you'll discover some awesome strategies to help you during tough times. But remember, even superheroes team up with friends to tackle tough challenges. If your distressing feelings seem like a big storm, and you're not sure how to handle them, that's when to ask for help. In the meantime, try these fun activities!

41. Radical Acceptance

Radical acceptance means that when things are tough or don't go as planned, you try to understand and accept them, even if you don't like them. Say to yourself, "This is how it is right now, and I'll do my best to handle it." Try to answer these questions to get an idea of how radical acceptance works:

- What was the distressing situation?

_____

- What happened before this?

_____

- How were you part of what happened?

_____

- How were others involved, too?

_____

- What can you control in this?

_____

- What can't you control?

_____

- What did you do when this happened?

_____

- How did you feel after your actions?

_____

- How did others feel about what you did?

_____

- What could you have done differently?

_____

- If you had just accepted the situation, how might things have turned out?

_____

42. The T.I.P.P. Skill

When you're feeling really upset, you can use the T.I.P.P. skill to help yourself feel better. T.I.P.P. stands for Temperature, Intense Exercise, Paced Breathing, and Progressive Muscle Relaxation.

- **Temperature** - Get a cup of cold water or hold an ice cube. You can even splash your face with cold water. This helps your body feel different and calms you down.
- **Intense Exercise** - Do some jumping jacks, run in place, or dance around for a little while. This helps your body release some of the strong feelings you're having.

- **Paced Breathing** - Take slow, deep breaths. Breathe in through your nose for a count of four, then breathe out through your mouth for a count of four.
- **Progressive Muscle Relaxation** - Tense and then relax different parts of your body. Start with your toes, then your legs, your tummy, your arms, and even your face.

43. The Self-Soothe Technique

When you're feeling really scared, worried, or angry, this technique can help you feel better. It's like giving yourself a big hug on the inside.

- **Find Something Soft:** Get a soft blanket, a cuddly stuffed animal, or even a cozy sweater. Hold it close to you.
- **Use Your Senses:** Notice things around you. Look at something pretty, listen to calm music or a favorite song, and maybe even smell something nice, like a flower or your favorite lotion.
- **Breathe Slowly:** Take deep breaths. Imagine blowing up a balloon inside your belly and slowly letting the air out. Do this a few times.
- **Talk to Yourself:** Tell yourself kind and gentle things. It's okay to feel scared or mad. You're safe, and you can handle it.

44. Fear vs. Reality

Sometimes, your mind can make things seem scarier than they really are. Like when you're watching a spooky movie and feel scared even though you *know* the monsters aren't real.

- **Draw or Write:** Get a piece of paper and draw or write down your fears. Maybe you're worried about a test or making a new friend.
- **Ask Questions:** Look at what you drew or wrote. Ask yourself, "Is this something that has happened, or is it something I'm imagining?"
- **Think of Facts:** Imagine you're a detective. Collect evidence about your fear. Have similar things happened before? What's the real chance of the scary thing coming true?
- **Talk It Out:** If you're not sure, talk to a grown-up or a friend you trust. They can help you see if your fear is a real problem or just a tricky thought.

45. The Worry Jar

Sometimes, worries can feel like a bunch of bouncing balls in your mind. The worry jar is like a special place where you can put your worries so they don't bounce around so much.

- Find a jar, a box, or even a container, decorate it, and label it "Worry Jar."

- Whenever you have a worry, write it down on a small piece of paper. It could be about school, friends, or anything else bothering you.

- Fold the paper and gently put it inside the jar. This is like giving your worries a place to rest.

- Choose a special time to open the jar and look at your worries each day, maybe after school or before bedtime.

- When you read each worry, think of ways to make it better. Sometimes, you'll realize some worries aren't as big as they seemed.

- After your worry time, close the jar. Imagine you're closing the lid on your worries until the next time you want to think about them.

46. Grounding Technique 5-4-3-2-1

This technique can help you feel calm and focused when your mind feels jumbled up. It's like using your senses as superheroes to bring you back to the present moment.

- **See (5 Things):** Look around and find five things you can see. Draw them in the given space. Maybe it's a colorful toy, a picture on the wall, or a book.

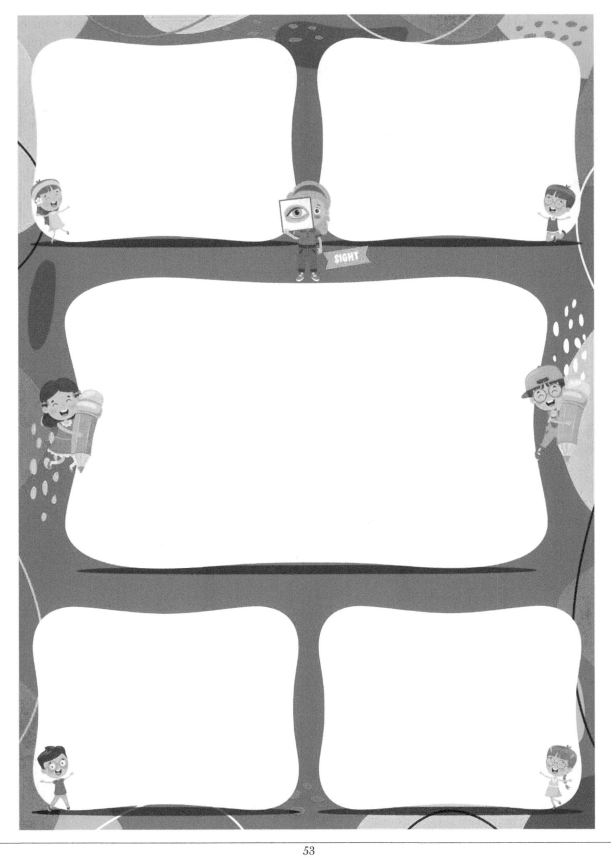

- **Touch (4 Things):** Find four things you can touch. Reach out and feel them with your hands, and write them down in the list. It could be a soft blanket, a smooth table, or bumpy tree bark.

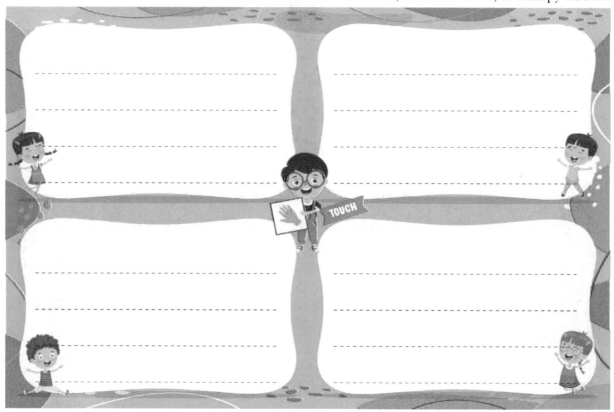

- **Hear (3 Things):** Listen for three things you can hear. Maybe it's birds singing, a clock ticking, or people talking.

- **Smell (2 Things):** Notice two things you can smell. Take a sniff and think about what it's like. It could be the smell of a flower, your favorite food, or even fresh air.

- **Taste (1 Thing):** Finally, think about one thing you can taste. It could be a snack you had earlier or the toothpaste you use.

47. Stress Map

When you're stressed, working towards a solution to your problem is hard. To deal with your stress, you first need to figure out what the cause of your stress is. Use this stress map to do so.

STRESS MAP

Where did it happen? Give some options.

Be more specific about the where.

Were you by yourself when it happened, or was someone with you?

When did it happen, the morning, evening, or afternoon?

----

48. In a Perfect World

Imagine a world where everything is just the way you'd like it to be. Picture a special place in your imagination where everything is super-duper awesome.

In a perfect world, I...

_____

In a perfect world, my family...

_____

In a perfect world, my school...

_____

In a perfect world, my teachers...

_____

In a perfect world, my friends...

_____

49. Positive Self-talk

Sometimes, you use not-so-nice words when you talk to yourself. You might say things like, "This is awful," or "I'm not good at this." But guess what? You can change those words to make yourself feel better and happier!

Negative Self Talk	Positive Self Talk
I'm terrible at this.	Mistakes help me learn and improve.

50. Cool Down

When your feelings are big and strong, like a bubbling pot, you need a way to cool down and feel better. It's like taking a deep breath for your emotions.

- **Recognize the Heat:** Imagine your feelings are like a hot, steamy pot. It's okay to feel that way, but you want to calm down.

- **Take Deep Breaths:** Close your eyes and take slow breaths. Inhale through your nose like you're smelling a flower, and then blow the air out slowly, like you're blowing on soup to cool it down.

- **Count or Imagine:** You can count to ten or picture a peaceful place, like a calm beach or a cozy blanket.

- **Talk to Yourself:** Use kind words. Tell yourself it's okay to feel upset, but now it's time to feel better.

- **Choose a Calm Activity:** Do something soothing, like drawing, reading, or listening to calming music.

Section 6: Understanding My Anger

When you can't reach your goal or get something you really want, it's normal to feel a little mad. Feeling angry is a part of being human. Everyone, even moms, dads, teachers, and friends, get mad sometimes. Sometimes people might tell you, "Hey, don't be mad," but it's not always as simple as that. Although everyone gets angry, it's not good to let your behavior get out of control because of it. For instance, maybe you got angry at your brother for being loud when you were trying to study. However, this anger becomes dangerous if you start to shout or throw things. This is why it's so important to manage your anger. To control your anger, you must understand what anger feels like.

Anger is a feeling you have when you're upset or frustrated about something. It's like a little alarm inside you that goes off when you feel like things aren't going the way you want. There are a few different types of anger and ways people show it:

Types of Anger:

- Regular Anger: This is when you feel annoyed or irritated about something small like a toy not working or a game not going your way.

- Big Anger: This is when something really upsets you, like when you're unfairly treated, or things don't go as planned.

- Sudden Anger: Sometimes, anger can come on suddenly, like when you're surprised or caught off guard by something.

Styles of Showing Anger:

- Yelling or Shouting: When people raise their voices to express their anger.

- Crying or Screaming: Some people might cry or scream when they're angry because they're feeling overwhelmed.

- Silent Anger: This is when someone gets really quiet and doesn't talk when they're angry.

- Physical Reactions: Sometimes, people might stomp their feet, clench their fists, or even hit something to let out their anger physically.

- Talking it Out: Instead of yelling, some people like to calmly talk about why they're upset.

- Taking a Break: Some people find it helpful to take a break, walk away, and calm down before talking about what's making them angry.

It's okay to feel angry sometimes, but it's important to find healthy ways to deal with it.

Your anger monster doesn't have to win.

https://freesvg.org/cartoon-red-monster-vector-image

51. Anger Sensations

Many physical and emotional sensations come with anger. From the given options, circle the experiences and sensations you feel when you get angry and separate the physical and emotional sensations:

- Clenched fists
- Hot face
- Wanting to hit someone
- Fast heartbeat
- Crying
- Scrunched face and eyes
- Pounding

- Wanting to hurt someone
- Throwing things
- Breaking things
- Exploding
- Frowning
- Growling
- Stomping
- Red face
- Tense muscles
- Gritted teeth
- Huffing
- Pounding heart
- Tearing up (like getting ready to cry)
- Slamming
- Yelling
- Sour feeling
- Tangled thoughts
- Stormy feelings
- Bursting

Physical Sensations	Emotional Experiences

52. Cause of Anger

Everyone gets angry for different reasons. To better manage your angry side, you first have to figure out why you're angry. Below is a list of things that make most people feel angry. Use the empty lines to jot down a time when each of these situations happened to you.

You don't get what you really want.

_____

_____

_____

Someone takes your stuff without asking.

_____

_____

_____

You think someone isn't being fair.

_____

_____

_____

Your plans don't work out as you thought.

_____

_____

_____

Someone says mean things about you or a friend.

_____

_____

_____

Something seems puzzling, and you're not sure why.

_____

_____

_____

53. Draw Your Anger

Draw a picture of what you think your anger looks like. It could be anything; a giant monster, a volcano, or even a small elf. This should not be a picture of you but a character. Once you're finished drawing, give this character a name, and use this name whenever you get angry.

54. Your Anger Triggers

An anger trigger is similar to a pot of water on the stove. When you turn up the heat, the water starts bubbling and sizzling until it boils over. Use these lines to jot down the five times you've felt really mad, even if you can't remember all of them right now. It's totally fine – you can come back and add more later on.

1. _____

2. _____

3. _____

4. _____

5. _____

55. Different Forms of Anger

From the list in the previous exercise, copy your anger triggers into the table below and write down different anger word next to them. Use the given word bank to better understand different types of anger.

ANGER WORDS BANK

NOUNS	ADJECTIVES	VERBS
Anger	Furious	Smouldered
Rage	Raging	Pounded
Fury	Frustrating	Exploded
Temper	Bitter	Erupted
Wrath	Jealous	Shook
Disgust	Breathless	Trembled
Contempt		Clenched

Situation	Anger Word

56. Anger Thermometer

As you've learned by now, one can feel different levels of anger. Use the given anger thermometer to express your anger to your parents, siblings, and friends. Cut it out and paste it in your room, on your diary, or keep it close to you.

What does it feel like?

Red hot all over. "Blood boiling".

I want to smash things up.

Seething inside. Hot. About to lose control.

Wound up. Everyone is annoying. I want to escape.

Itchy, uncomfortable. Feels like everything is going the wrong way.

Soft. Relaxed.

What helps?

Get away from people. Punch my punching bag. Play your favorite anger music.

Go for a run.

Move to a different environment. Listen to a podcast. Eat, drink.

10-minute yoga workout. Get outside.

57. Anger Journal

Use the following format to record when you get angry and how it affects you. This can be a great way to determine how to improve your behavior.

1. Draw how you felt when you were angry.
2. Write why you got angry in that situation.
3. Draw how big your anger was on a scale.
4. List ways to calm down when angry.
5. Write three steps to follow when angry.
6. List things that make you happy and calm.
7. How to apologize and forgive.

58. Angry Thoughts

Do you remember what you were thinking just before you started feeling angry?

_____

Are there any specific thoughts or ideas that tend to pop up when you're getting angry?

_____

59. Anger Reaction

What do you typically do or say when you feel angry?

_____

Do you think your reactions help you feel better or make the situation better?

_____

60. Anger Management

Can you recall a situation where you felt angry but managed it in a good, friendly, and positive way?

_____

What did you do differently in that situation that helped you handle your anger?

_____

Section 7: Transforming My Hulk Anger

You have probably heard of the famous Marvel character "The Hulk" – he's one of the heroes of the Avengers. He's this super awesome guy who transforms from a brilliant scientist named Bruce Banner into a humongous, green-skinned powerhouse known as the *Hulk* whenever he experiences intense anger or emotional stress.

Just like the Hulk, you can transform your anger.

Maybe you've heard of his cousin "She-Hulk" as well. They both get their superpower from anger. However, when they need to transform back into their normal selves, they ultimately have to gain control over their anger. If these insanely angry characters can transform their anger, so can you! Maybe you can even relate to the Hulk when you get mad. Does your brain ever go, "Hulk smash!!" whenever someone tests your patience? If so, you're not alone. Lots of kids struggle to manage their anger. But don't lose hope; you can surely transform back from the insane green giant back into your usual self with just a few tips.

61. Cognitive Restructuring

Cognitive restructuring is all about changing your negative thoughts into positive ones. When something breaks, Hulk usually wants to SMASH the person who broke it. But, if the person is someone he cares about, like his friends (the Avengers), then Hulk stops and thinks, "Maybe I can fix it or find a new one." As a result, his anger disappears, and he turns back into his usual self. Imagine if he got mad at Thor; that would be a sight to see, right?

62. D.E.A.R.M.A.N Technique

You've already been introduced to the D.E.A.R.M.A.N. technique, but how can you use this to control your anger? Well, the basics remain the same, but the specifics do change. Consider a Hulk story to understand this.

THE AVENGERS MEETING

The Avengers are gathered around a table, discussing a recent mission gone awry. Iron Man, Captain America, Black Widow, Thor, Hulk, and others are present.

Iron Man (frustrated): "Hulk, you can't just smash your way through everything! You nearly destroyed that entire facility!"

Hulk's anger starts to rise, but he takes a deep breath, remembering the D.E.A.R.M.A.N. technique he learned.

Hulk (calmly): "Tony, I noticed you're upset about the damage I caused, and I understand. I felt like smashing things was the best way to handle the situation."

The other Avengers look surprised by Hulk's controlled response.

Black Widow (curious): "Hulk, we appreciate your strength, but there's a better way to coordinate our efforts."

Hulk (assertive): "I want to be a team player, and I'd appreciate it if we could work together to find a solution. Maybe we can come up with a plan before charging into the next battle."

Captain America nods in agreement, and Iron Man realizes Hulk is making a valid point.

Iron Man (nodding): "Alright, Hulk. Let's agree to coordinate better and come up with a strategy before jumping in."

Hulk's tense expression starts to relax.

Hulk (reassured): "Thanks, Tony. If we do that, we can be even more effective."

The Avengers continue their discussion, this time with a more collaborative approach, planning their next mission carefully."

Remember, young heroes, even the Hulk, know that expressing feelings and finding common ground can save the day on and off the battlefield.

63. S.T.O.P.P. Technique

The S.T.O.P.P. technique has also been previously introduced. So, consider how to use this technique when you're getting mad. Imagine playing your favorite video game and trying hard to get to the next level. But every time you almost make it, you lose and have to start over. This can make you feel super frustrated and angry. That's when you can use the S.T.O.P.P. technique to help you handle your anger.

S - Stop: Press pause on the game or put down the controller. Take a moment to stop and take a break.

T - Take a Breath: Breathe in slowly through your nose, like you're smelling your favorite snack, and then breathe out slowly through your mouth, like you're blowing away a pretend cloud.

O - Observe: Look at the screen and notice how your character is still cool, even if you're stuck. Look at your feelings and see how anger might be taking over.

P - Pull Back: Imagine you're a game designer looking at the situation. Maybe there's a different strategy you can use or a hidden trick you missed.

P - Practice What Works: Think about what you can do to improve. Maybe you can try a new approach.

64. Progressive Muscle Relaxation

Hulk gets angry and tense all the time, but guess what? Even Hulk needs to chill sometimes. How does he do that? With *progressive muscle relaxation*! Here's how he does it:

- **Fist Smash:** First, make your hands into super tight fists like Hulk when he's ready to punch. Squeeze them as hard as you can, counting to three, and then... relax! Let your hands go all loosey-goosey, just like when Hulk turns back to Bruce.

- **Strong Arms:** Next, pretend you're Hulk and flex those arm muscles by making your arms super straight and strong. Count to three again, then let go and let your arms become soft and floppy.

- **Squeeze Your Face:** Now, scrunch up your face like Hulk when he's grumpy. Make it really tight, count to three, and then release. Let your face become calm and smooth, just like Bruce Banner's.

- **Hulk Hunch:** Hulk sometimes stands really tall and strong, but then he gets tired and slumps over. So, arch your back like Hulk, count to three, and then relax, letting your back become comfy like a pillow.

- **Strong Legs:** Pretend you're Hulk stomping around with super strong legs. Tense those leg muscles for three seconds, and then let them relax and feel all wobbly.

65. Positive Affirmations

Everyone needs encouraging words and *positive affirmations* from time to time. These come in especially handy when you're feeling super angry at something or someone. Take a look at these affirmations brought to you by none other than Hulk and She-Hulk!

POSITIVE AFFIRMATIONS

I AM Special

TODAY
I
CHOOSE
TO
THINK
POSITIVE

I AM Happy

I
CAN
GET
THROUGH
ANYTHING

I
GET
BETTER
EVERY
SINGLE
DAY

I AM Kind

I AM
AN
AMAZING
PERSON

I AM Creative

I AM Brave

I
BELIEVE
IN
MYSELF

I AM loved

GOOD
THINGS
ARE
GOING
TO COME
TO ME.

I
CAN BE
ANYTHING
I
WANT
TO BE.

I AM Smart

IF
I FALL,
I WILL
GET
BACK
UP AGAIN

I AM Beautiful

66. Anger Playlist

An Anger Playlist is a list of songs that can help you calm down and feel happier. Music is like magic for your emotions! When you're angry, listening to your favorite songs makes you feel better. If you don't have any idea where to start, give these songs a go:

- Count on Me
- Brave
- True Colors
- Don't Worry, Be Happy
- You've Got a Friend in Me
- What a Wonderful World
- Hakuna Matata
- A Whole New World
- Three Little Birds
- Rainbow

67. Calm Down Technique

Small physical movements can help distract you and calm you down when you feel your anger rising up and out of control. One of these techniques is shredding paper. Collect a bunch of papers that you and your family are fine with tearing up. Rip the papers into tiny pieces and have fun trying out different types of paper to discover which one feels the best to tear. If you want, you can even write down things that are bothering you, making you sad, or causing you to be mad, and then tear up the paper and toss it away. It can feel really good to do that! Here are some ideas for papers you can tear up:

- Printer or computer paper
- Old school worksheets that you don't need anymore
- Pages from a newspaper
- Phone book pages
- Used notebooks or notepads

NOTE: Make sure that you don't tear up something that belongs to someone else!

68. Block Out Noises

Have you ever felt like there was just too much noise around you, and you wished you could make it all go away, especially when you can't think straight because of your anger? Sometimes, all the noise can feel like a jumble that's hard to sort out. Guess what? There are special headphones that can make all the noise disappear! And if you can't get those, you can use earplugs or even just cover your ears with your hands for a little bit. Taking this quiet time can help you feel calm and relaxed.

69. Dear Anger

When you feel really angry, find a quiet spot to write a letter to your anger. Start the letter with Dear Anger. Tell it how you feel when it shows up, like when you got mad because your game got messed up. Share what happens when your anger takes over, like shouting or breaking things. Say you want things to be better and not messy. Ask your anger if you can work together to fix things. This letter helps you talk about your anger and figure out how to handle it in a good way.

70. Hulk Anger Story

Learn the importance of controlling your anger with a story featuring the Hulk and She-Hulk.

HULK, SHE-HULK, AND LOKI'S UNLIKELY TEAM-UP

In the heart of a bustling city, the Avengers had gathered at their headquarters, discussing recent events. Loki, the mischievous god, had caused a chaotic ruckus with alien invaders not too long ago. Tensions were high, and Bruce Banner, also known as the Hulk, was especially furious.

Loki strolled in, his sly grin intact, but he was met with Hulk's thunderous glower. "Hulk smash!" Hulk roared; his massive green fists ready to pummel Loki.

"Wait, Hulk!" She-Hulk, Bruce's cousin, leaped in. She stood between the raging Hulk and the smirking Loki. "Hold on a moment!"

Hulk growled; his anger barely contained. "Move! Hulk needs to teach him a lesson!"

"Wait!" She-Hulk repeated firmly, raising her hands. "Loki might have something we need."

Loki's grin widened. He conjured a small, glowing artifact and held it up for everyone to see. "Indeed, cousin. This bauble could save the day."

Hulk's rage flickered, curiosity replacing it. She-Hulk turned to him. "Bruce, remember our breathing exercises. Inhale, exhale."

Reluctantly, Hulk took a deep breath, mimicking She-Hulk's calming technique. Slowly, his colossal form began to shrink, the green hue fading.

Loki chuckled. "Well done. Your soothing tactics might be worth something."

With Hulk's anger diffused, Loki explained how the artifact could neutralize an impending alien threat. Reluctantly, the Avengers agreed to work with Loki, and an uneasy alliance formed.

As the team ventured to the battleground, Loki's clever tricks and the Avengers' combined strengths thwarted the alien invasion.

When the dust settled, and victory was achieved, Hulk gave Loki a nod of begrudging respect. Loki smirked, acknowledging the unspoken truce.

With the day saved and newfound understanding, Loki vanished with a flourish, leaving behind a city in awe and a team of Avengers, including a calmer Hulk, standing strong.

And so, an unlikely partnership formed, proving that even the fiercest emotions can be controlled, and sometimes, the unlikeliest allies can save the day.

The end.

Section 8: Mindfulness and Relaxation

Do you sometimes feel that your mind and body are disconnected? Your body might be at school while your thoughts wander back home. Or you're at the dinner table chatting with your family, yet your mind is still thinking about a problem you had on the playground earlier. It can make focusing a bit tricky, right? Well, in this section, you will be exploring the world of your mind and how you can give it a helping hand to stay on track. Think of your mind like a muscle. You can flex your focusing abilities with a little practice and watch them grow stronger. Soon enough, you'll find it easier to tune into whatever you want. This is called being mindful, and it's pretty awesome!

Mindfulness is like a special superpower that helps you pay close attention to what's happening right now. It's like being a detective of your own thoughts and feelings. When you're mindful, you're like a calm explorer on a big adventure, noticing all the little details around you. It's about taking a moment to breathe and really focus on how you feel, what you see, and what you hear. Mindfulness helps you stay calm, happy, and present in the moment, like a magical secret to feeling good inside.

Relaxing is something you should do every day.
Videoplasty.com, CC BY-SA 4.0 <https://creativecommons.org/licenses/by-sa/4.0>, via Wikimedia Commons https://upload.wikimedia.org/wikipedia/commons/thumb/e/e1/Black_Man_Relaxing_on_the_Beach_Cartoon_Vector.svg/512px-Black_Man_Relaxing_on_the_Beach_Cartoon_Vector.svg.png

71. Facts-Feelings-Mind Activity

Gather up a jar, some rocks, sand, and a cup of water. This activity will teach you how to be mindful. First, imagine your mind is like a jar. The rocks are like the important facts. Before your feelings come in (like the sand), you want to put the facts in your mind jar. If you let your feelings take over first, there won't be space for all the facts!

Now, think of a situation. Who, what, when, and where – those are the facts. Write them down! Imagine your mind jar again. Put only the facts (rocks) in the jar. See the spaces between the rocks? That's where your feelings (sand) can go! Dump out your jar and keep the rocks nearby. Quickly fill the jar with sand. Try putting the rocks back in. Do they fit? Usually, it's harder because of the sand.

Try again! Get your rocks ready and put some in the jar, saying the facts out loud. Then, pour the sand around the rocks, saying your feelings. You might need to shake the jar gently to fit the sand around the rocks. If there's space left, pretend the water is like help. It's like talking to someone for advice or support. Even if you think there's no room, try adding a little water. Did you notice you could fit it in? That's a reminder that you can always get a bit of advice or support, even if you're not sure you need it.

72. The G.I.F.T Technique

Imagine you're playing with your friends at the park, but you start feeling sad because you remember a time when you got in trouble at school. That's something from the past, making you feel down in the present. Or maybe you're worried that you might not do well in a test next week. That's a future worry, taking your attention away from the fun you're having right now. But wait, here's where your magical G.I.F.T. comes in! Let's say you remember to use G.I.F.T. You realize that feeling sad isn't about what's happening at the park. So, you use the secret code:

G - Get

I - Into

F - Focusing

T - At this moment

You take a deep breath and look around. You notice the green grass, your friends laughing, and the slide you want to go down. You realize that you're doing great right now, and all those sad or worried feelings can take a little break. By using your G.I.F.T., you bring your attention back to the park and all the fun things you can do.

73. Mindfulness Practices List

Make a special list of things you need to get done. Write down how you feel and what you think about each task. Then, come up with cool ways to stay focused while you do these tasks so you'll have more time for the fun stuff you want to do later.

Tasks	Thoughts	Feelings	Mindfulness Skills	Reward
Homework	Homework is boring. I want to watch a movie.	Angry, frustrated, distracted	G.I.F.T. technique	I can watch my favorite movie

74. Mindfulness Meditation

Find a cozy spot and take a couple of deep breaths to relax. Wait for a moment, then open your ears to the sounds around you. Are there cars on the road? Maybe birds are singing, or a garbage truck is making noise. Now, focus on the sounds inside the room you're in. Can you hear a sound machine humming? Listen closely – is the light making a soft buzz? Is the clock ticking away? Then, pay attention to your own body sounds. Can you catch the sound of your tummy rumbling? Do you notice any signs of a headache? Be mindful of all sensations.

75. Yoga

Yoga and mindfulness go hand in hand to help you feel calm and aware. They're all about reducing stress and paying attention to what's happening now. Try these fun and easy yoga poses:

- Strong Warrior Pose

- Sneaky Cobra Pose

- Comfy Easy Pose

- Silly Seal Pose

- Curious Downward Dog

- Playful Camel Pose

76. Mind Jar

When your mind feels scattered and you're having trouble focusing, a mind jar can help you calm down. You can use it before starting your homework, when you're a bit annoyed, or simply need to unwind. Here's what you need for a basic mind jar: a container, warm water, and glitter paint. Choose a container that's right for you, like an empty soda bottle or a plastic jar. Warm water works best – it helps the water and paint mix nicely. Glitter paint is great because it keeps the glitter contained and makes cleanup easier.

Put some glitter paint at the bottom of the jar, just enough to cover it. Pour in warm water, close the lid tightly, and shake it well. You can also experiment with other ingredients like hair gel, corn syrup, or glue to keep the glitter afloat. You can add things like Legos, glitter, small stones, or even glow-in-the-dark stars to your jar for extra fun. This little jar can be your secret tool to help your mind find peace.

77. Take a Mindful Walk

Every time you take a walk, whether it's at home or school, you can turn it into a special mindful walk. Before you start, prepare your mind to notice all the amazing things around you. While you walk, focus on what you can hear, see, feel, and smell. Keep your senses awake and alert. It's okay if other thoughts pop into your head – just gently bring your focus back to what you can sense right now. Try doing this for about 5 minutes – it's a fun challenge to stay tuned in to your senses!

78. Mindful Breathing

Deep breathing techniques are perfect for practicing mindfulness and clearing your mind. This technique can also come in handy when you want to control your emotions and reactions. Adding a touch of organization and fun can be helpful when learning to take deep breaths. Shapes offer a simple method to count your breaths in and out. Just follow the shape with your finger as you breathe to keep track of your rhythm. Try the box breathing technique to practice mindfulness:

Imagine you have a magic box that you can use to control your breathing.

- Breathe In (4 seconds): Pretend you're blowing up a balloon inside your box. Breathe in slowly through your nose for a count of 1, 2, 3, 4.

- Hold your Breath (4 seconds): Imagine your balloon is floating inside the box. Hold your breath gently for a count of 1, 2, 3, 4.

- Breathe Out (4 seconds): Now it's time to let the air out of your balloon. Breathe out slowly through your mouth for a count of 1, 2, 3, 4.

- Pause (4 seconds): Imagine your empty balloon resting in the box. Pause for a count of 1, 2, 3, 4.

You can repeat these steps as many times as you want. It's like a mini-vacation for your mind.

79. Drawing Your Thoughts

Creating drawings can be a super cool way for you to practice mindfulness. Pick your favorite colors and try these fun drawing exercises:

- **Rainbow Doodles:** Draw a big, curvy rainbow on your paper. Fill each colorful stripe with patterns or tiny drawings. As you draw, focus on the lines you're making and the colors you're using.

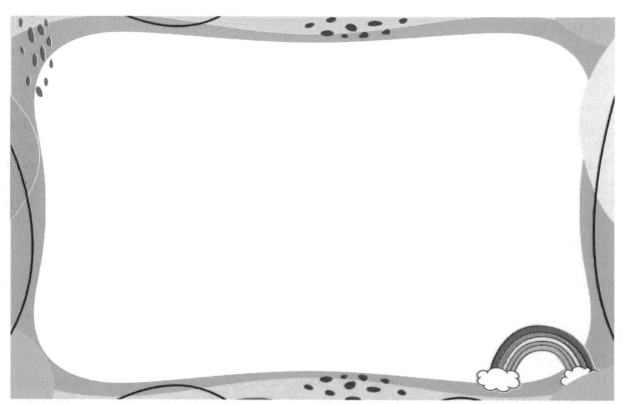

- **Zentangles:** Start with a simple shape like a square or a circle. Then, fill it with small, intricate patterns. Let your hand move slowly and steadily, paying attention to each detail you add.

- **Nature Sketch:** Find a cozy spot outside or look at a picture of nature. Draw what you see – it could be a flower, a tree, or even a bug. Pay close attention to the shapes and textures.

- **Emotion Art:** Pick an emotion, like happiness or calmness. Close your eyes and think about what that emotion feels like. Then, draw whatever comes to your mind, using colors and lines that express that feeling.

80. The R.A.I.N. Technique

The R.A.I.N. technique is a cool way for kids to practice mindfulness when dealing with tricky feelings. Here's how to use it:

- **R - Recognize:** First, notice and recognize the feeling you're having. Maybe it's worry, anger, or something else. Give it a name and say, "Hey, I see you!"

- **A - Accept:** It's natural to have feelings. Accept that it's normal to feel this way sometimes. Don't try to push the feeling away. Imagine giving it a little hug.

- **I - Investigate:** Ask yourself some questions. Why do you feel this way? Is there something that triggered this feeling? Try to understand it a bit better - be a detective.

- **N - Not Identify:** Remember, you're not the feeling. You're just feeling it. It's like trying on different hats - you're not the hat, but you're wearing it for a while. So, you're not the feeling, but you're feeling it right now.

Section 9: Mindset Makeover

Negative thinking is like a little cloud that tries to cover up your sunshine. It might whisper things like, "You can't do it," or "It's too hard." Have you ever had thoughts that made you feel like you're not good enough? Well, that's something called "self-sabotage." It's like accidentally tripping over your feet while trying to run. But don't worry; you can learn to step over those obstacles and keep going. Another thing you need to keep an eye out for is an ANT - Automatic Negative Thought. These thoughts are like little bugs in your mind that try to make you feel bad. There are different types of ANTs:

- **Black-and-White Thinking:** Seeing things as only good or bad, like having only vanilla or chocolate ice cream.

- **Focusing on the Negative:** Only thinking about the bad stuff, like noticing one dot on a beautiful painting.

- **Labeling:** Putting a label on yourself, like saying you're bad at something. But you're more than just one label!

- **Blaming:** Pointing fingers instead of looking at the whole picture, like blaming rain for a picnic indoors.

- **Fortune Telling:** Thinking you know the future, like saying you'll fail a test before even studying.

ANTs (Automatic Negative Thoughts)

ANTS are like little bugs that sometimes crawl into your mind. These bugs tell you negative things that might not be true. For example, if you're trying something new, an ANT might whisper, "You can't do it; you'll fail." But guess what? You have the power to squish those ANTs! You can say to yourself, "I can try my best, and that's what matters." By squishing ANTs, you can feel more confident and positive.

PETs (Positive Encouraging Thoughts)

PETs are like friendly pets that live in your mind and help you feel happy and strong. They say nice things to you, like, "You're really good at trying new things!" or "You can handle challenges." When you have PETs in your mind, they help you feel better and remind you of your strengths. So, whenever you catch an ANT, you can replace it with a PET to keep your mind positive and strong.

This section is all about shifting your mindset from the negative to the positive. A mindset makeover! Just as a caterpillar transforms into a beautiful butterfly, you can transform your negative thoughts into positive ones.

81. Turn ANTs into PETs

Imagine your thoughts are like ants. When you notice a negative thought, catch it like you're catching an ant! Then, think about a positive way to see the situation. For example, if you think, "I'm not good at math," catch that thought and turn it into "I can improve my math skills with practice and help."

ANTs	PETs

82. Fact or Feeling?

When you feel sad or worried, take a moment to think. Are your feelings based on real facts or just how you're feeling? Sometimes, we feel sad even when things are going well. Try to find evidence that balances out your feelings.

Problem	Fact	Feeling

83. Positive Affirmation Mirror

Stand in front of a mirror and look at yourself. Say three positive things about you. It might feel strange, but it helps you see yourself in a positive light. For example, say, "I'm a good friend," "I'm creative," and "I can learn new things." Write these down as well.

1. _____
2. _____
3. _____

84. Gratitude Gems

Every day, write down three things you're thankful for. It could be big or small things, like a yummy snack, a fun game, or spending time with your family. Focusing on the good stuff helps you feel happier overall.

1. _____
2. _____
3. _____

85. Turn Problems into Puzzles

Imagine problems as puzzles you can solve. Instead of feeling upset, tell yourself, "This is a puzzle I can figure out!" Just like you enjoy solving puzzles, you can enjoy finding solutions to challenges, too.

86. Growth Garden

Fill out this growth garden worksheet and color it. On the roots, write down challenges you've faced. On the leaves, write down something positive you learned from each challenge. Just as a plant grows strong with water and sunlight, you grow wiser with challenges and learning.

87. Happy Helpers

Think of something kind you can do for someone else. It could be helping your sibling with their chores or drawing a picture for a friend. Doing nice things for others makes them happy and makes you feel good! Write these down.

1. _____
2. _____
3. _____

88. Positive Role Models

Think about someone you look up to who stays positive even when things are tough. It could be a family member, a character from a story, or a real-life hero. What do you like about how they handle challenges? Try to act like them when you face difficulties. Write their name and draw a picture of them.

89. My Optimism Jar

Decorate a jar with colors and stickers. Write down good things that happen to you or things you're proud of on colorful notes. Fold the notes and put them in the jar. When you're feeling down, pick a note from the jar to remind yourself of positive moments.

90. Vision Board

Collect magazines or print pictures from the internet. Look for images that make you happy or things you want to achieve. Glue these pictures onto a big piece of paper to create a "Vision of Joy" board. Use the template given below. Hang it in your room, and look at it when you want to feel inspired and positive!

Name:

GOALS

School

DREAMS

GOOD VIBES

health

Family and Friends

Positive

Section 10: I Love and Respect Myself

Imagine a sky full of stars, each one twinkling in its own way. Just like those stars, every person on this planet is unique and special. You are a star, too, shining with your own light. No one else can be you, which makes you absolutely amazing! Think about how you love and care for your friends and family. You're always there to cheer them on, offer a helping hand, and share a smile. Guess what? You deserve the same love and respect from yourself! You can be your own best friend, your number-one supporter, and the person who loves you the most. Close your eyes for a moment and think about everything that makes you awesome. Maybe you're a fantastic artist, a great soccer player, a wonderful friend, or a curious learner. These qualities are treasures within you. Embrace them, celebrate them, and be proud of them!

91. Strengths Spotlight

Write down three things that you're really good at. These are your strengths – the things that make you amazing! Now, think of a time when you used each of these strengths. How did it help you or others around you?

- **My Strength:** _____
- **How I Used It:** _____
- **My Strength:** _____
- **How I Used It:** _____
- **My Strength:** _____
- **How I Used It:** _____

92. Compliment Collage

Grab some old magazines, scissors, and glue. Look through the magazines and cut out pictures or words representing your talents and qualities. Glue them into this collage template to create a colorful collage that celebrates YOU!

COMPLIMENT COLLAGE

93. Daily Self-Appreciation Journal

Every day, write down something you appreciate about yourself. It could be something you did well, a kind thing you did, or a quality you like. Remember, even small things count.

Today, I appreciate _____

94. Strengths Interview Game

Find a friend or family member and take turns interviewing each other. Ask about strengths and positive qualities. Share what you learned with each other. Create your very own fan club!

- **I interviewed:** _____

- **One strength I learned about them:**

_____

_____

95. Imaginary Superpower

Imagine you have a superpower that represents one of your qualities. Draw a picture or write about it below. How does this superpower help you in your daily life?

My Superpower: _____

How It Helps Me:

_____

_____

96. Personal Achievement Timeline

Create a timeline of achievements – big or small – that you're proud of. Draw pictures or write about them in the boxes below. Look at how far you've come!

PERSONAL ACHIEVEMENT TIMELINE

97. Self-Esteem Affirmation Cards

Write down some positive things about yourself on these cards. Keep them where you can see them, and read them every day. Remember to believe in yourself.

Affirmation 1: _____

Affirmation 2: _____

Affirmation 3: _____

98. Celebrating Successes

Think about something you achieved recently. It could be finishing a book, helping a friend, or doing well in a game. Write about it and how it made you feel below.

I achieved: _____

How it made me feel: _____

99. Role Model Reflection

Who's a person you admire? Write their name and the quality you share with them. You have awesome qualities, too, just like them!

Role Model: _____

Shared Quality: _____

100. Strengths Bingo

Look through this bingo list and check off qualities that describe you. How many can you find? You're like a treasure trove of amazing qualities!

STRENGTHS BINGO

treats others with kindness	knows how to solve problems	good at planning and organizing	brave	looks out for well-being of others
works well with others	makes others feel included	asks good questions	forgives others	good at communicating
patient with others	helps others who are stuck	FREE	listens closely to others	manages time well
focused	curious and likes learning new things	considerate of others' feelings	has a growth mindset	respectful of others
works well independently	honest and trustworthy	sets and accomplishes goals	positive attitude	creative

Bonus Section: The Forgiveness Tree

Sometimes, people make mistakes or do things that might hurt your feelings. When you forgive them, you give them a chance to make things right. But guess what? Forgiveness is not just for them - it's also for YOU. It helps you feel free from those heavy feelings and gives you a fresh start. Forgiveness is like a magic potion for your heart. When you forgive someone, it means you're letting go of any anger, hurt, or grudges you might be holding onto. It's like giving your heart a big hug and saying, "It's okay; I'm moving forward." Here's a fun activity that can help you learn more about the concept of forgiveness.

Create something truly special - your very own Forgiveness Tree. Think of it as a magical tree that helps you understand forgiveness. First, print and cut out the Forgiveness Tree template. Glue the branches onto the trunk and add the roots at the bottom. Now comes the fun part - write down the names or descriptions of any negative feelings you've had lately on the leaves and attach them to the branches. Look at your Forgiveness Tree and imagine those negative feelings gently floating away, leaving you feeling lighter. This tree reminds you that you can let go, heal, and forgive. Keep it somewhere you can see it, and whenever you do, remember that just like a tree grows and changes, you too can grow and let go.

LEAVES:

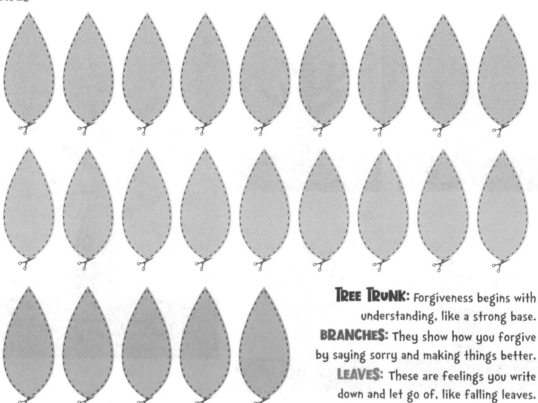

TREE TRUNK: Forgiveness begins with understanding, like a strong base.
BRANCHES: They show how you forgive by saying sorry and making things better.
LEAVES: These are feelings you write down and let go of, like falling leaves.
ROOTS: They're the values that help you stay strong and forgive.

BRANCHES:

TREE TRUNK:

BRANCHES:

ROOTS:

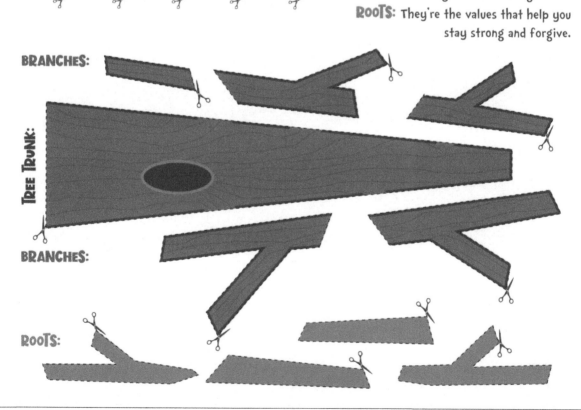

THE FORGIVENESS TREE

Thank You Message

Wow, you did it! You finished this workbook, and you must be over the moon with excitement! Your hard work and enthusiasm are truly impressive.

Guess what? Your skills treasure box is now overflowing with all the cool stuff you've learned. You've shown some real superstar skills, and seeing you shine is fantastic.

Always remember, you're like a superhero with endless abilities. Keep exploring, learning, and trying new things – there's no limit to what you can do.

Also, every challenge you face is like a puzzle to solve, and you have the smarts and courage to solve anything! As Dr. Seuss once said, "The more that you read, the more things you will know. The more that you learn, the more places you'll go."

So, keep that curiosity alive, ask questions, and keep learning. Whether you're painting a masterpiece, building a tower of blocks, or learning about the stars, you're creating your own unique adventure.

Always believe in yourself because you're capable of achieving amazing things. As Winnie the Pooh wisely said, "You are braver than you believe, stronger than you seem, and smarter than you think."

The world is full of possibilities just waiting for you to explore.

A huge thank you for being an inspiration and a wonderful learner. The world is a better place with you in it!

Keep rocking and keep being amazing!

CERTIFICATE
OF ACHIEVEMENT

Presented to

FOR

Date:

Signed:

Self-Care Enchantment

Coping Potions

Emotion Surfing

Mindfulness Magic

Thought Wizardry

Problem-Solving Elixir

Communication Spells

Check out another book in the series

References

Anger worksheets for children. (n.d.). Therapist Aid. https://www.therapistaid.com/therapy-worksheets/anger/children

Ayeni, M. D. (2023, March 29). 25 dialectical behavioral therapy activities to raise emotionally intelligent kids. Teaching Expertise; dontan. https://www.teachingexpertise.com/classroom-ideas/dbt-activity/

Behavioral Tech. (n.d.). Dialectical behavior therapy for children. Behavioraltech.org. https://behavioraltech.org/dbt-for-children/

Compitus, K. (2020, October 1). What are Distress Tolerance Skills? Your ultimate DBT toolkit. Positivepsychology.com. https://positivepsychology.com/distress-tolerance-skills/

Courtney E. Ackerman, M. A. (2017a, February 3). 25 fun mindfulness activities for children & teens (+tips!). Positivepsychology.com. https://positivepsychology.com/mindfulness-for-children-kids-activities/

Courtney E. Ackerman, M. A. (2017b, March 14). 20 DBT worksheets and dialectical Behavior Therapy skills. Positivepsychology.com. https://positivepsychology.com/dbt-dialectical-behavior-therapy/

Courtney E. Ackerman, M. A. (2017c, December 29). Interpersonal effectiveness: 9 worksheets & examples (+ PDF). Positivepsychology.com. https://positivepsychology.com/interpersonal-effectiveness/

Day, N. (2021, April 24). Distress tolerance: What is it? How to help children develop it. Raising An Extraordinary Person. https://hes-extraordinary.com/distress-tolerance-children

DBT interpersonal effectiveness skills: The guide to healthy relationships. (2017, August 18). Sunrise Residential Treatment Center. https://sunrisertc.com/interpersonal-effectiveness/

DBT tools. (n.d.). Mindful Teen. https://www.mindfulteen.org/dbt/

Dialectical behavioral therapy for children. (2022, July 18). Hillside Atlanta - Behavioral Health Support for Youth, Adolescents, and Their Families. https://hside.org/resources/learn-about-dbt-c/

Emotion exposure : (2018, December 30). DBT; Dialectical Behavior Therapy. https://dialecticalbehaviortherapy.com/emotion-regulation/emotion-exposure/

Garey, J., & Emanuele, J. (2016, January 28). DBT: What is dialectical behavior therapy? Child Mind Institute. https://childmind.org/article/dbt-dialectical-behavior-therapy/

Idaho Youth Ranch. (2020, July 10). 5 DBT skills to help your kids manage stress. Youthranch.org. https://www.youthranch.org/blog/5-dbt-skills-to-help-your-kids-manage-stress

Jennie Lannette, L. (2022, October 7). 25 best expressive emotions games for teaching feelings and skills. Counseling Palette. https://www.thecounselingpalette.com/post/emotionsgames

Kerrie, J. (n.d.). DBT interpersonal effectiveness skills. Mental Health Center Kids. https://mentalhealthcenterkids.com/products/dbt-interpersonal-effectiveness-skills

Ld, S. K. W. (2019, February 15). DBT may help regulate emotions - smart kids. Smart Kids -Smart Kids. https://www.smartkidswithld.org/getting-help/emotions-behaviors/dbt-may-help-regulate-emotions/

Linehan, M. (n.d.). Interpersonal effectiveness skills. Dialectical Behavior Therapy (DBT) Tools; JW-Designs. https://dbt.tools/interpersonal_effectiveness/index.php

Marie, S. (2022, May 2). Anger management for children: Can you teach emotional regulation? Psych Central. https://psychcentral.com/health/anger-management-for-kids

Mindfulness activities for children. (n.d.). Therapist Aid. https://www.therapistaid.com/therapy-worksheet/mindfulness-for-children

Sutton, J. (2021, June 11). Anger management for kids: 14 best activities & worksheets. Positivepsychology.com. https://positivepsychology.com/anger-management-kids/

Swetz, H. (2021, August 21). Emotional regulation activities for kids. The Homeschool Resource Room. https://thehomeschoolresourceroom.com/2021/08/21/emotional-regulation-activities-for-kids/

Vallejo, M. (2023, April 28). Dialectical behavior therapy for kids. Mental Health Center Kids. https://mentalhealthcenterkids.com/blogs/articles/dbt-for-kids

(N.d.). Choosingtherapy.com. https://www.choosingtherapy.com/mindfulness-for-kids

Made in United States
Orlando, FL
07 December 2024

55046295R10063